WATCHA

Deep Vellum Publishing
3000 Commerce Street, Dallas, Texas 75226
deepvellum.org · @deepvellum

Deep Vellum is a 501c3 nonprofit literary arts organization founded in 2013
with the mission to bring the world into conversation through literature.

Support for this publication has been provided in part by grants from the National Endowment
for the Arts, the Texas Commission on the Arts, the City of Dallas Office of Arts and Culture,
the Communities Foundation of Texas, and the Addy Foundation.

Paperback ISBN: 9781646053070
Ebook ISBN: 9781646053223

LIBRARY OF CONGRESS CATALOGING-IN-PUBLICATION DATA:

Library of Congress Cataloging-in-Publication Data

Names: Villarreal, Stalina, author.
Title: Watcha / Stalina Emmanuelle Villarreal.
Description: Dallas, Texas : Deep Vellum, 2024.
Identifiers: LCCN 2023055976 (print) | LCCN 2023055977 (ebook) | ISBN
9781646053070 (trade paperback) | ISBN 9781646053223 (epub)
Subjects: LCGFT: Poetry.
Classification: LCC PS3622.I493985 W38 2024 (print) | LCC PS3622.I493985
(ebook) | DDC 811/.6--dc23/eng/20231201
LC record available at https://lccn.loc.gov/2023055976
LC ebook record available at https://lccn.loc.gov/2023055977

Cover art by Jorge Galván Flores
Designed by Emily Mahon
Interior layout and typesetting by Andrea García Flores

PRINTED IN CANADA

WATCHA

STALINA EMMANUELLE VILLARREAL

DEEP
VELLUM

Dallas, Texas

Listening involves a reciprocity of energy and flow; exchange of energy; sympathetic vibration: tuning into the web of mutually supportive interconnected thoughts, feelings, dreams, vital forces comprising our lives; empathy; the basis for compassion and love.

—Pauline Oliveros

Contents

1.

From the ear to the eye, I have reinterpreted the practice of Deep Listening as established by Chicana composer and musician Pauline Oliveros to create a Deep Watching manifesto. The aim is to listen to artists' work and create a sense of community. Although watching can be a solitary affair, I understand watching art to be communication between the artist and the viewer. In visual art, the artist does not have to be present for reciprocity, but I suggest that ekphrastic poetry is a way to talk back to the artist. I hope that Deep Watching by means of ekphrasis will enable celebration of communities.

I was upset by anthropologist Arlene Dávila's words in her book *Latinx Art: Artists, Markets, and Politics*: "Latinx art and artists are almost entirely shut out from 'the market' as it is increasingly narrowly defined around the world of galleries, auction houses, and art fairs, the primary spaces that lead artists to accrue a market history that adds economic value to their subsequent work." While *Watcha* started out as a broader endeavor, I narrowed my focus down to Latinx art, including Afro-Latinx art. Although some Latinx artists identify as Indigenous, I also wanted to add Native artists who are in conversation with Latinx artists. My purpose is to give more visibility to these artworks and artists.

By Deep Watching, I borrow from Oliveros's notion that hearing is involuntary and that listening is voluntary, but I extrapolate this concept to assert that seeing is involuntary, while watching is voluntary. Similarly, I apply her definitions of focal and global listening to focal and global watching. Focal watching is when the observer concentrates on details, whereas global watching provides context.

Most of the ekphrastic poems contained in this volume remove the lyrical *I* so that the reader can insert their own *I* in my eye; I intend for the gaze to be a witnessing of the artwork. Any quotations without attribution are documentary poetics that draw from the source of the artwork itself. Watching becomes a hyperbole.

Further, my photographs serve for the viewer to watch my watching. Oliveros coined the term Quantum Listening for the listening to listening, so *Watcha* seeks to practice Quantum Watching.

Shadow Initiation

A History Removed

Clay,
　nonferrous metals,
　　　　steel,
　　　　　oil paint,
　　　　　　acrylics,
　　　　　　　pastels,
　　　　　　　　graphite,
　　　　　　　　　marker,
　　　　　　　　　　pen,
　　　　　　　　　　　photos in a darkroom.

　　　　　　　　　　　With the mark
　　　　　　　　of a hand, a gesture and texture—
　　　　　oceanic forms for my Gulf
　　　of Mexico frontera with lentil
　dents on porcelain, with my heels
on the porcelain.

Mythology does not apply.

                                     Logic turns inward.

                                                        Sensuality becomes abstracted.

My sculpture professor said, "White bread is wheat bread in the toilet," yet my photography professor said, "You are spiritual," because I pointed the camera toward the light.

2.

My fascination with visual art perhaps is rooted in my failure to sustain visual art as a career.

I get caught between my destination and origin. I often get asked, "Where are you from?" I recall trying to flirt with a drag queen who was a white Whitney Houston impersonator—she was dancing with some kicks, so I tried dancing along using my capoeira kicks—and she rebuked, "Are you illegal? Let me see your driver's license." Al escucharla, la audiencia empezó a irse del bar. Ella trató de salvarse y dijo <<te pregunté por tu edad, ¡déjame ver tu identificación!>> Pareció que era una agente.

Los niños regiomontanos me llamaban <<Stalina gallina come gasolina>> which I translate as "Stalina hyena eats ammonia." Rimar sin sentido era su manera de cantinflear. Al cruzar la frontera mis bravucones me llamaban <<Stalina wiena>> lo equivalente a una salchicha en Spanglish ¡a female wiener! porque era flaca, y antes de la pubertad, no tenía las curvas para darme una forma no salchicha. Los machos eran mayores y altos; luchaban cara a cara contra mí. Al quejarme, los adultos no me creían y decían que era una chiflada. El silencio se convirtió en mi enemigo, cuyo cachete me gustaría abofetear. Untitled: Why I became a poet.

Cruzando The Crossing

Watcha

1

"Hispano"   Soap.
      Esto no es oro   sculpture,
soap steps   lead   to a wall,

ivory   to ochre   shades,
      stacked   body   size
but stand

with potential   to be handheld,
      but in an art space   untouchable,
each soap branded   "HISPANO."

Violette Bule   critica
      al neoliberalismo   y   capitalismo,
lack of gold,   but a product

of consumerism,   españolparlante
          in a country   where   *Hispanic*,
coined   by the Nixon   administration,

el derecho   a self-determination,
          inmigrantes   and   citizens co-live
pero   el privilegio   divide

a la Latinx   population,   y el jabón
          de la exposición   no limpia.

2

Woman carries   the weight of dirty
          dishes and dried spaghetti   in *Dream*
America.   Ojos cerrados.

Bule's curator   Surpik Angelini
          reminds us,   "Antes de la estética
está la ética."   Ojos abiertos,

the same burden   on the same
    woman's shoulders,   except the weight
is an incomplete—

3

The ethics   of the aesthetics
    brings irony to   *Slam the Dreamers*
postcard.   Una mujer   holds a rifle

with one hand,   cotton candy
    with the other.   French fries   cover   her
crotch   as she sits   on a picnic table.

"in guns   we trust,"   says the hotdog
    bun on the U. S. A.   flag sign.

4

Un laberinto   vertical   *Dream la Bestia*
    maps the migrant   route   from Guatemala
to the United   States   on a stowaway train:

long, yellow   fabric   with embroidered
    animations,   the lost and found   of imagery,
busy,   excessive,   necessary to see,

empezando   abajo and going
    up. In Tapachula   soldiers use batons
and rifles   en contra de la gente.   A man eats

sandía, y otro fuma   and drinks   alcohol.
    At Arriaga   a man   controls   mujeres
like marionettes.   Farther by the train tracks,

on the way   to Ciudad Ixtepec,   mujeres
        raise their arms   as babies   and   infants lie
next to knives   and machetes   and adults, naked,

are slaughtered.   Gente escapa,
        hold and climb   la bestia train.   At Estación
Lechería,   coyotes rape   women, beyond

the guitar,   tambores,   maracas, underwear
        hangs from a tree,   underneath and behind,
naked figures   lie, sit, prance,   or fuck

as uniformed   police approach
        with binoculars, guns, or   batons, la patrulla
in their pickup   trucks threaten. Closer

to the border   un vaquero   kills a figure
        using underground   tunnels. Maquiladoras
where the route forks to Tijuana,   Juarez,

y Matamoros.   More tunnel holes,   one person
          zapped by the Statue   of Liberty's red
laser eyes from the other side of the wall.   Entre

la frontera y el muro,   cowboys shoot
          and lasso humans   Seres humanos.   The wall
tiene estereotipos: graffiti by MS13,

Mexico with McDonald's   arches, and two
          figures   with sombreros, an anchor,
and a ladder   up to the barbwire.   Drones fly on both

sides.   Beyond the wall, three
          Klansmen stand,   one   with a salute
toward the Las Vegas   and Hollywood   signs. Prisoners

line up to enter   la cárcel with a smokestack
          that releases cash   instead of smoke,   to enter
the Payomatic   building. A six-armed   Mickey

Mouse serves   the food industry   without a smile.
     Smiling is   Eddie Murphy   in his *Coming*
to America outfit by the satellite   and surveillance

cameras. Skyscrapers behind   the WALMART, BEST
     BUY, and   COCA-COLA   signs.

Passport Interrogations

Suspended in air floating,
    two figures flee diagonally
        wearing bush-printed hoodies,
            shorts, and legs to camouflage,

near la migra who is likely to ask,
    where did you go? How long
        did you stay there? Do you

have relatives there? La migra
    with painted red and blue skin,
        sunglasses, cap, and brown collar.

An acrylic bird crashes into
    a circular landscape of a river,
        while brick façades drape

over a wooden peg. *Where did*
    you go? How long did you stay
        there? Do you have relatives there?

The fleeing figures have rasquache leaves
        for a face, hands, and feet, while Mexican

Indigenous fabric dolls have human faces
        and bodies, except for the deer doll, all

in a box. The atmosphere of *Alkanzíyya* exudes
        a call para humanizar. In a video Jorge
                Galván Flores tosses a brick

to a second video of a laborer,
        the two screens disjointed
                at a diagonal, your eyes move.

Chico MacMurtrie and Amorphic Robot Works (ARW)'s
Kinetic Tunnel Sculpture

When the arms unfold and extend
into arches, you can walk through, pass.
A gallery attendant commands, "Don't
touch!" as they monitor the museum-
goers who cannot resist the marvelous
tunnel robot. To regulate entry is to control
the passage, to treat the espacio like
a frontera, except the arches only last
a moment before they close back up
and entrap you. Poet Arnoldo García
believes this sculpture is a detention
center, but because upon closure
of the arms, you must escape, almost as
if the robot itself is the border patrol that
allows entry sometimes, but not always.
Tunnel escapes are processional whereas
the sculpture has immediacy. The metaphor
of this specific tunnel, according to the curator
Robb Hernández, is a lot more like
an "'abduction' by an alien force." As

such, this control is intergalactic, and
its physicality makes it real, not fiction.
I walk and see flashes of white stripes.

Invader de Aztlán

Sergio Hernández questions why the U.S. government called immigrants "aliens" when the word means extraterrestrials.

Aztec hieroglyphs on the base of an extraterrestrial's head encased in glass, glowing—an androgynous relic with closed eyes and a remarkable headdress almost holds the base with three-fingered hands.

Art historian Ray Hernández-Durán argues the painter draws from the 1953 movie poster *Invaders from Mars*, which has a similar extraterrestrial head in a bubble; one of the aliens has closed eyes.

Invader de Aztlán translates to "Invader from Aztlán" as well as "Invader of Aztlán," the enemy from within and them vs. us.

Artist Henry G. Sánchez claims that Hernández was inspired by a Star Trek character with a bulbous head as well as an episode in which "a head is held in suspended life under a glass dome."

El programa enseñó actos no discriminatorios al tratar a los seres de varios planetas y galaxias con dignidad.

Mapping Borders

Laura Drey weaves both
simply yet intricately

    a palimpsest and patchwork
    of burlap, polyurethane,

        and produce twist ties.
        The import and export

           of products reflect
           migration. "CILANTRO"

                "BULB," "PRODUCT
                OF MEXICO." Texture

                    of the bias and netting.
                    Contrast of colors, each

                        marking a region for the eye
                        and stomach of landscape:

a map of what holds edibles
sabrosos, llamativos, abstractos.

Feminicidio fronterizo

Nabil Gonzalez's massive, cascading
sand and abundant name tags:
Lourdes Gutiérrez Rosales

y las desaparecidas. Maquiladoras gone.
No body y el alma ¿por dónde estará?

Discs of illusional eyes, eyeliner,
and plucked eyebrows sobre la arena

del desierto, terrain shaped
like a wrinkled skirt.
¡Ni una más!

Lo que subsuma Celeste De Luna

Candlelit, *Our Lady*
        of the Checkpoint, relief

print, protector contra la migra
        stands on telescopic eyes

with barbed wire alrededor.
        Where did you go? How long
            did you stay there? Do you

have relatives there?
        La calavera observa that death

amenaza our Anzaldúan "conocimiento"
        of the unknown beyond a bridge.

Where did you go? How long
        did you stay there? Do you
            have relatives there?

Where a child anchors
       fenced borderlands
              with wind turbines y flores.

3.

I'm fourth-generation immigrant. My great-grandfather was a guest worker who—lo que aprendimos a través de DNA tracing—started a second family in the United States. My grandfather moved to this country as a skilled laborer when my mom was a child, also 1.5 generation in the United States. She moved to Mexico as an adult and came back after a decade, when I was a child, part of the 1.5 generation también.

Stasis is impossible when so much fluctuates. Yet a sense of belonging calls for a stay. Finding a place does not always feel at home. Coming home seems to be more of an action rather than a noun, yet a noun is contingent on the verb. En español el sujeto suele ser implícito, sobre todo cuando escribo sobre el yo.

Durante mi adolescencia me huí del barrio para estudiar. Regresaba durante mis vacaciones o cuando estudiaba en la universidad en Austin, regresaba a Houston ciertos fines de semana. Después que falleció mi abuelita, visitaba a mi abuelito a pie. Al caminar, más detalles lucen por mi barrio Magnolia. Pensaba que la canción "Velouria" de Pixies decía "my Magnolia" pero en realidad the singer doesn't, aunque todavía la canto de mi manera. Una de las veces que mi abuelo me corrió de su casa, le tomé una foto a una familia cruzando la calle.

And what of the children? A mother is trusting enough to allow a stranger to take a picture? How does one define barriers? I could not help but think of the children. How trusting would the mother be when they got older? Would they, too, leave the barrio or come back or stay?

Unknowing, I thought about artworks that are about place. To what degree is belonging appropriate, and what political implications relate to place?

Casa

Flooded Memoria

Stephanie Saint Sanchez's
    Tip Drop: Time Machine—Before the After

a vintage
    1974 zenith
        television rayada
            la pantalla with image
                de la casa, also known
                    as Penwood Studios starred

"A MILLION YEARS AGO AND
    YESTERDAY" written on
        the screen, as time has lapsed

since Hurricane Harvey, a soundscape
    patchwork of songs, sounds, and words
        from a ghost channel in the barrio:

"Time to change;
    you've got to rearrange;
        what you gonna do?"

George Lopez joked,
    "I can't breathe!
        I can't breathe!"
            years before
                Eric Garner and George Floyd.

Displaced but present in what has passed
    in the past, leading to a ruptured future.

"Whoa, whoa!
Our house,
    family
        know
      a time,
        take a chance
            and face the wind

Harvey

same people . . . come back."

Comentario Social, Textile Style

Outside, sepia and color
    portraits, ancient pero fuertes,
        standing or sitting, stoic
            people of color on washed ochre,
                golden, chartreuse, or fuschia textile collages,
                collages hanging from a clothesline,
                familial memorias e historias,
                    from a Southern, Gulf Coast,
                      Afro-Xicana perspective, a very
                      dimensional, queer
                        weaving, craft
                        de tela e
                          imágenes.

Inside, loom círculos of gold,
    yellow, and purple abstract quilt
        on a wall, labor. Leticia Contreras's fiber
            art, and a body labyrinth of blue oceanic
                cyanotype on fabric, sunlit negative space.

Deconstructed Patriotism

Homage yet parody
        of Latin American abstract
expressionism, Gabriel

Martínez uses found fabric,
        discarded rags and clothes,
from Houston streets
and sidewalks, buttons
        and zippers removed,

fabric handstitched on
        stretched canvas, Marxist
materials on high art.

        Compositions range
from synthetic to cotton. Both
        natural and unnatural fibers
like polyester, Lycra, nonflammable threads.

One angular cotton composition,

          fabric breathable and soft,
yet with a history of slave

          labor, with red, white, and blue,
stripes, some solid blue
          and white pieces, all stitched
with red and blue thread,

colores de representación:
               United States of America,

abstracted straight angles and curves,
               some patches, no flag or stars,
settler procesado a mano.

Bianca Mercado's *Fusterlandia*

A quilt of fifteen squares,
recycled fabric of images
and letters: Afro-Latinxs,

pets, and many
slogans: "ME MUERO /
CONTIGO PERO / NO

ME MUERO / POR TI."
A sense of solidarity yet
independence, a cause.

"SALUD / AMOR / PAZ."
A purpose compassionate.
"SI MALO ES REGALARSE /

PEOR ES VENDERSE / MUCHO
MENOS PRESTARSE / ES MEJOR
TENERSE." To protect oneself

becomes a necessity. "EL PEZ NO
SABE / QUE EXISTE EL / AGUA."
The unknown can necessitate.

"SOCIALISMO / O MUERTE."
Mocking authoritarian regimes.
Hard content on soft fabric.

4.

Muralist Judith Baca argues that figurative art provides legibility. I do not deny this, but I believe that abstract art is legible as well. The difference is that figurative art accounts for the power of norms, not necessarily better, but there, existent. This reminds me of literary genres. When I lived in the Bay Area, I often saw people read on public transportation. I was the annoying neighbor who would interrupt asking, "What are you reading? Do you like it? Why do you like it?" Most of the answers appeared to be reruns of a show I call *Memoir, Because I Can Relate.*

Una de las veces que mi abuelo me corrió de su casa, me fui a pie y le tomé una foto a dos niñas en sus triciclos, y la madre se puso enojona:
"Don't take pictures of my kids!"
"They're on the street; it's legal for me to take their picture."
"Well, I don't want you to."
I could not help but wonder what happens to the countless children from my neighborhood. Attitudes from mother to mother seem to vary greatly.

My own mother had a distaste for visual arts; she said that if the amount of people who went to art openings could show up to protests, political movements could be more powerful. Becoming a Studio Art major in college was the most rebellious act I could do.

The Return of el Retrato

Laura Aguilar's *Latina Lesbians* Series, Black and White, Gelatin Silver Prints

1

Judy a stunning futch woman, a "'professional lesbian'"
facing you seriously, parted lips, testimonio: "work
together for equal protection under the law" to "accept

increasing diversity in our community," standing
in front of a "STOP AIDS" poster: "groups . . . responding
to end . . . the epidemic." Buttoned stripes and leaf print.

2

Yolanda una guapa futch woman, testimonio: "My latina
side informs my lesbian side with chispa & pasión"
with a "powerful promise," looks away "with a vision." "¡!Y qué?!"

3

Carla an attractive butch mujer, testimonio: "mother encouraged"
profession as "a court reporter" but "became a lawyer," seriously
stares at you, black leather unzipped, hands by hips, elbows winged.

4

La combinación de palabras con imágenes forma la hibridez,
cuya curiosidad alerta a ambos lados del cerebro. La fuerte
imagen de una mujer se ve de lejos, pero para leer hay que acercarse.

Fade Away: Desaparecer

Nery Gabriel Lemus's offset print of eighteen
men, some Latino, some African American,
swapping barbers but ending with similar
hairdos: a few with haircuts with edge
ups, some skin fades, some have
tapers, some plain tapers, others a
taper fade, or high and tight.
They are framed por un fondo
checkered by autumn umber
and burnt umber. None
face you, entre
ellos, él who
side-eyes
you.

Los Jefitos de Jef Huereque

After Luis Valdez

Shadows in front
of a blue landscape

flattened, perpendicular
to a red and white checkered

floor, *My Parents
in Their Matching*

Zoot Suits, a portrait
of two, a standing

couple, la pachuca
y el pachuco, oil

on canvas, their prominent
pompadours and drapes:

they don the ombré
hues of local color:

mostly warm,
some cool:

entacucharse
con carlangos

y calcos, apa
wears tramos,

ama, a skirt.
Ready for

el borlo. ¡Órale!
Watcha!

Chale.
Con safos.

5.

During the pre-selfie era, I hardly posed in front of a camera. Once, when I was twenty-four, I still had explosive acne but took a picture anyway. It was one of the times when my abuelito kicked me out of his home, and afterward someone had couch-like van seats by their house—I occupied their space a few moments to rest, reflect, and continue my Magnolia Park walk home. So what if my beliefs clashed with my elder? La única persona que me ha explicado la religión en una manera que entiendo y quizá estoy de acuerdo es Gloria Anzaldúa. Explica que las diosas aztecas fueron víctimas del machismo y hay que recuperar sus feminismos. No rezo a esas diosas, pero las ideas anzaldúanas afirman la identidad liminal que llama <<nepantla>>, un espacio fronterizo espiritual en que hay una transformación. Soy nepantlera. O quizá nepantlera agnóstica.

I disagree with the vast amount of people who believe that self-portraiture is self-indulgent. It is a way to observe how you look at yourself, and it is not always pleasant. My first painting professor asked me if I felt whole because I cropped myself so much, and the truth is that I did not. By the time I took a photography class, I wanted to correct myself, attempt to look more whole. Only now do I accept that my fragmentary lifestyle is acceptable.

Mirroring

Non-abuelita Grandma

"You get love by video," says Jillian Mayer
        to her unborn grandchild. A newer form
                of familial communication that records

in case of death or in the event of aging,
        in an age freeze, or communication
                across distances, borders, and times.

In *I Am Your Grandma*,
        instead of the stereotype of abuelitas
                in the kitchen, and although kitchen-

table feminisms do exist, Mayer
        se disfraza de grotesque, fantastical beings:
                humongous wigs, fun fabrics of costumes,

a shiny mask with metallic outfit, clown-
        like figure, chain mail and disc headdress,
                a crying baby mask:

difference between the grandma and child,
opaque mask with wig, mask
with eggshell shine and a tall-crown top hat,

covered with miniature disco balls
and cones, hardened wig and makeup, once
with black joker lips.

Virtual cariño in absurd but intriguing imagery.

The Female Gaze Facing the Self:
Tina Hernandez Self-Portraiture

1

Herstory and Chicana
symbolism, like
"*virgen/puta* (whore)
dichotomy"
that Anzaldúa terms,
with half face
maquillada
and skin, half face
sin maquillaje
and a religious
rebozo.
Or as the dead
of the *Self-
Regeneration*
series.
*Allegory
of a Chicana* series
appropriates like sensual
skin and la muerte.

La medaojo is Medusa's parody
with an oval frame and eleven eyes
at the ends of snake-like braids
and their shadows, goth eye makeup,
and an upper lip with a snare.

3

La Malinchola, a hybrid between
Malinche and a chola, with calla lilies
in the background, like a Rivera painting.

A red bandana braided, floral headdress, and a white
tank top and a gold Malintzín neckless, dark lipstick.

She wears hoop earrings and a necklace
that has a yoni bead between leg beads.

She intimidates shy people
like me but is stunning. ¡Chingona!

Tropical Baby (Self-Portrait)
Bebé Tropical (Autorretrato)

Carolyn Castaño painted
                    herself,
acrylic on canvas, glitter
            on the afro,

small round mirrors on the afro
                        so that the hair
is you, the hair is we,
            the hair is I

the viewer, round mirrors
                        como flores,
flores como tú, flores como
            nosotres, flores

como yo, and rhinestones,
            on the eyelashes,
glitter on the black outline
            of geometric

shapes in the background.
The light
glimmers,
a gorgeous
self.

A Photographic Progression of the Self

Isaac Reyes's self-portrait cropped,
cabeza volteada to profile, looking away

self-portrait sideways with sticks,
plumas e hilo en el fondo

self-portrait of a face, hands, and arms
desapareciendo into a grainy, green background

self-portrait hanging from a tree holding
un paraguas con persona sentada on a bench below

self-portrait of a bouquet wrapped around the neck
autorretrato screaming with distorted lighting

self-portrait as a piggyback hummingbird on leaves in a bedroom
autorretrato in colorful flamboyant makeup

self-portrait both in drag and cis
autorretrato at the doorway of home.

6.

In *Borderlands/La Frontera*, Gloria Anzaldúa refers to "a language with terms that are neither *español ni inglés*, but both." She describes several languages that Chicanos speak, some of which are included in these ekphrastic poems: standard English, slang English, standard Spanish, Tex-Mex, Chicano Spanish, and "*Pachuco* (called *caló*)."

Inconformistas que se llaman caifanes nacen del concepto pachuco de rebeldía, para recuperar su manera de ser, disfrazarse de su estilo con un look llamativo, bailar el swing con un ritmo sincopado, definir sus propias proclividades, estar en contra de lo contrario. Los caifanes de la película *Los caifanes* de Carlos Fuentes se colaron donde no se permitía pero también cuidaron a la protagonista. Los integrantes de la banda rockera Caifanes contrastaron a la música tradicional de les padres, pero también negaron el idioma del imperialismo; mientras la ironía del lenguaje en español reforzaba el colonialismo del lenguaje, ya que decir *no* se opone en la lengua.

Oliveros argues, "It is the nonlinear carbon chaos, the unpredictable turns of chance permutation, the meatiness, the warmth, the simple, profound humanity of beings that brings presence and wonder to music." I am a fan of nuance.

Some works I love are not portraits but are suggestive. The abstraction implies the body, or the action of videos suggest an interiority. With the former, shapes or process-oriented work can be very bodily. With the latter, interpersonal interaction can have intrapersonal retrospection.

Beyond Más Allá

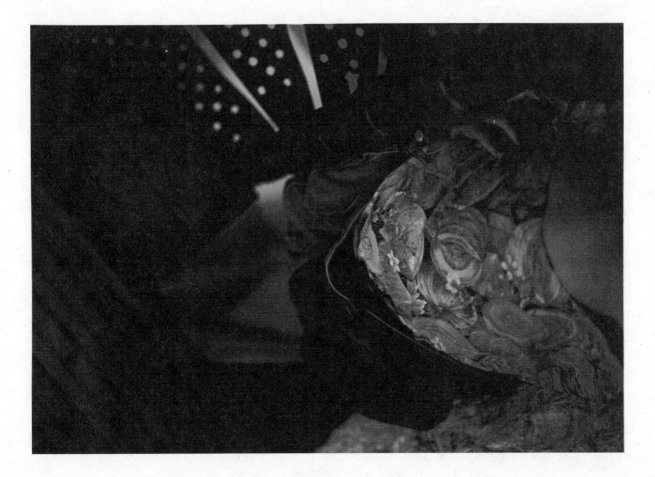

Consciousness y la mestiza

Nepantla in parts, begins
    with an epigraph: "In
        America they make you

    believe Spanish is a lovers
language in truth it is
a romantic kidnapping,"

    said by Elisabet
        Velasquez. "Intro" serpent

        eye and multiple Karen
    Martínez heads until

    one filmmaker and actor
Martínez holds
una pintura. Lineage

    unfolds a handheld víbora.

In "Auto Da Fé" Martínez
      holds a mother idol La virgin
            de Guadalupe and crushes

      her fiction and figure. "La

      Piedad en el Desierto"
    shows a woman's border
crossing. A snake eye and
SIN FRONTERAS water

jug. Un nopal asalta upon a fall.

     "Flor de Jaguar" embraces
   a lesbian couple, la macha
con un machete, sharpening

while sitting on a bed until . . .
   tenderness.
         Flower of the underworld.

Martinez's *Nepantla* looped

with her *Malinalli*, a reclaiming
of Cortés's slave
by birthing in freeing
ancient smoke
entre mujeres, entre
mujeres, entre mujeres
and a contemporary cigarette.

Erick Zambrano's Sculptural Composition
of Gendered Visceral and Cerebral Abstraction

Tejida, Tejido, Tejide
all genders woven. The *-e*

        in *Tejide* includes nonbinary
        folks, while *Tejida* refers

to a mujer, whereas *Tejido* means
un hombre. Together they are

        woven without gendered
        assumptions as to who

weaves repeatedly
with Tyvek, for sealing homes,

        intricate pieces entre dos
        duct-taped palos, at diagonals,

with the base held down
by loose concrete, Tyvek ends

nailed to wood, with the middle
net woven: yellow, red,

and multicolored plastic, wire, copper.
Behind, "CAUTION" tape also

woven, red and white strips
woven tight. In the meshes,

tagua nuts or *vegetable ivory*
from a homeland, a rite

of manual labor, the migrant
Latinx experience, laborious

cuts, the striping of business,
repetitious weaving. Materials

found in parking lots, Tyvek
and nuts. Collected cariño,

embraced genders. Luscious
textures, meditated y amades.

Physical Space of *Bodies of Color Cuerpos de Color*

Pottery can survive lava yet
is fragile to handling and dropping.

Seven vessels,
only one brown vase is

symmetrical; the rest
of the pottery bends at the

belly. Two misshapen brown
vessels lie down instead

of resting on their feet. Two black
vases have narrow necks and

mouths, one with bulbous
shoulders. Wayne Perry uses

terra cotta and black stoneware
to show the variety of skin

tone in Black and Brown
comunidades. All have endearing

proportions, as in ceramics when
measurements and math create

fuzzy feelings. Their movement
shows ephemera and viscera.

¿Quiénes son "my people"? La respuesta feminista sería que no hay ninguna diferencia entre nosotres y elles; a la vez, hay que reconocer contrastes para diversificarnos. Sólo sé que entre estos extremos, quisiera que les muertes vivieran, ya que no se me escapa la morbididad de ser sobreviviente de cáncer y sobreviviente de mi intento de suicidio. Me dedico a les muertes y las personas vivas que lamentan la muerte.

In an act of self-annihilation, I once attempted suicide. I had been misdiagnosed and was taking a high dosage of prescribed amphetamine stimulants. I was wired and read nonstop, but all I marked in a translation of Sor Juana Inés de la Cruz was the word "pulverized." Lo que me salvó: no tenía cuchillos filosos para cortarme las muñecas con éxito; bueno, el verdadero éxito es que estoy viva. My proximity to death that night has given me an emotional connection to the dead and what's dead.

Some art survives the artist, while some artists survive the art.

Tócame: I'm Touched

Desire to Touch el mundo de Mundo Meza

1

The gray nalgas of a male nude
            facing you as homoerotically
                        as the muscular back

                        and bent arms, his head
            turned to the side. Face effaced,
dark geometric shapes crumpled,

like painted architectural smoke from
            the head of beauty during the AIDS
                        monochromatic epidemic.

                        The intimacy of a bedroom removed
            by a blank background on canvas,
do not touch.

2

An artist whose work realiza
        una belleza, a desire to touch
                is difficult to resist.

3

                Blankness of a canvas highlights the figure
        de un autorretrato that disappears
with rough primer expressionism

over a delicate face, blotted out by large
        strokes. Plaid-shirted, the torso also erased
                by whiteness. A black smudge accompanies

                the background on the surface.
        The only colors: hair and skin.
Gestures prevail over precision.

4

Portrait Study of white-collar class,
            no color, just a black tie, and striped
                    jacket without lapels. Bust intact, yet

                  face abstracted, full of busy lines,
       shapes and patterns. No mouth
or eyes or nose or ears to sense.

5

Painted designer platform shoes with five faces
            on each foot. Dark eyeshadow, with each face,
                   eyeliner, and lipstick, an icon surrounded

                  by green glitter and rhinestones. The shiny
       shapes of green serve as a headdress, collar,
and dress patterns.

6

Indiscernible to the viewer whether the head
      of the *Merman with Mandolin* bears oceanic mutations
            behind his head where you see two circles with concentric

            dots as well as two floral-like shapes by the ear and also
      two phallic forms at the back of the head—or perhaps
he is in front of an asymmetrical animal—or has a plant halo.

7

Rayas de colores form the skin of *Jef Huereque*,
      pastel on paper. The asymmetrical bust of a man's
            profile, with head lowered: chin and shoulder undulate.

8

Two *Sweet* pallid women, one with pink flamingos
on her dress, except one flamingo protrudes
from the dress to bite, upside down, the threads

netted, as depicted in acrylic on canvas, by the base
of the second woman. Both grab their hips, while
their legs disappear.

9

Ink on paper, "CyCLONA HAS BEEN HiDiNG
in tHE DESERt." Her androgynous body has no hands;
instead, her wrists have animal heads. An ambiguous

person stands behind to the side. On the other
side, the writing is reflected as if a mirror is
the background. By the thigh, a hatted face: "MUNDO MEZA."

10

A drug trip inked on paper, two bodies
sprawled on the floor, one mouthing a hose
connected to a bong. The red background

surrenders a heavenly face and stars, two faceless
bodies, one with curved wings and a straight beak,
the second has swirls instead of a head, layered.

11

Inked sketch of a snake at the feet of three
dismembered bodies and one whole
person with hair upwind yet stiff.

12

Print of three planes of ten persons,
        two at the front bottom, cloaked in black,
            one lying across the other in shadow, light

            legs bulging with high heels. Beside lay
        two, one leaning against the black cloak,
the second below on floor as if dead.

Another between the bottom and middle
        planes, lies in part fetal position, part haphazard
            as if dead or asleep. Two nudes lounge in the middle

            plane, on a radiating zigzag blanket outdoors.
        Next is father and child in Mesoamerican attire,
instead of a Medieval mother and child, busy

patterns surrounding. A distant trans bystander in
the top plane, wearing thigh-high leggings,
bikini underwear, yet a hat and whip.

13

Wig Shop's central figure is a drag queen
in a dress printed with human figures
discombobulated by the creases, and a dog hovering

in front, as the drag queen ascends a staircase.
The dog is spouting blood from
the mouth. Red marks
in the direction of a person on the side in black.

Death as a Fashion Statement

"I will wear death before I get killed."
—Ángel Lartigue

1

At street risk of being
a victim of a hate
crime, a queer
nightclub protege
a un equipo trans.

La voz alta of a song
removed, an androgynous
garment drapes over
the dancer; tied petri dishes
align, covering el cuerpo.

Under undergarments,
private parts se esconden.
The dancer covers her face

with a pink organic vapor
respirator. Black sleeves without
a shoulder, black gloves and heels.

The amber circles exist as a 1.75
inch radius of microorganisms:
arte científico de borrego

blood agar, cultivated human
cadaver fungi, necro-bacteria,
maggot exoskeletons.

A Xoloitzcuintle leads spirits
to the underworld and takes
el equipo to the dancefloor where they
dump buckets of burial site materials.

Strangers dance around the powder
dust, composed of human and animal
parts. Against categorization, like trans.

The team collects the remains
with *Operation Psychopomp* gear,
gloves and covered shoes. A rite

documented: two
photos and a rhythmic film.
In the aftermath, an installation

of stillness pulls gravity
from a hanger, as the petri-
dish garment gets grounded
by vulture feathers encircled in pink.

2

Por los siglos de los siglos

"UNDETERMINED SEX," "SACRED HEART," "DISTURBED"
"SOIL DEPRESSION," "TRANSMITTED," "DUST," "DEVOTION"
"VULTURE FEATHER," "CIELOS," "ROOTS"

"ABSORBED FEMUR," "EMBRUJADX," "ENTRE FRONTERAS"
"EL TIEMPO PASA Y NO PERDONA," "PELVIS," "ENTRE MUNDOS"
"ALMA," "SCAVENGED RADIUS."

Ángel Lartigue's *Operation
Psychopomp* saved gloves that touch.

Despite a Catholic
end, Aztec
mythology begins.

Pilgrimage of archeological
maps of exhumed muertes
texanes from a body farm. Aztec
god of death Mictlantecuhtli,
a conduit for the underworld,

cuida a les desconocides y nuestres
seres querides. Drawings of a mariposa,

hormigas, larvae, and maggots are so
stylized, that bugs se ven hermosos.

3

Muertx

At Moody Park, a dead naked
trans body lies in a puddle.

The live one with flowers
in hand, purple petals amid

neutrals tones of nature
and a dark asphalt trail,

a duality in which Lartigue
photoshops herself to be two,

where human cadaver and
the still alive but grieving are one.

8.

Doubling can create mutual action. El coro de Pauline Oliveros se enfoca en la comunicación aural, y participo al leer poesía entre pausas o en conjunto con algune vocalista que canta sonidos no verbales o vocaliza ruidos sonoros. Expulso palabras no digeridas sino sí dirigidas hacia la audiencia. No es vomitar conceptos. Es escupir saliva sabrosa para mojar el aire con ondas sonoras que viajan hacia cerebros a través de los oídos. La colaboración intercambia resonancia fonética entre nosotres, una amistad establecida por nuestras voces. A veces empiezo yo o quizá elle con la voz magnífica, pero a veces somos un dúo. O un eco. Lo importante es escucharnos y respondernos, hasta finalizar con un ritmo mutuo.

Doubling can create a multiplicity, or at least a gathering. Vengo de una familia política que cree en la justicia social y la consciencia colectiva; es a través de mi servicio a la gente, que he logrado integrarme a grupos, sobre todo con la solidaridad de las causas políticas.

What is mutuality? I noticed the workers, and they noticed me. They found humor in my admiration for their labor, and I now laugh at their laughter.

My family believes in union work. At one point, my mother worked for the AFL-CIO, my brother works for IBEW, and I once worked for SEIU undercover to see under which conditions managers paid their workers. We were a union family, and because my mother was a Chicana activist, I grew up not being able to eat California grapes during the boycott, also boycotting Wal-Mart because of the labor conditions their workers endure. We did this together in solidarity with workers, although I failed to recognize that we were not alone.

What my mom failed to see in art is that art is part of activism, or artivism. Artivism has been a part of many social movements, and art can serve as a political consciousness. She admitted that the Chicano Movement included a cultural renaissance. This duality is a doubling.

Throughout my mom's years an activist, award after award, she recognized the collective efforts to mobilize for social justice and that help is communal.

Action Juntes

Artist's Proof Print for
Origins of the Gay Rights Movement

Judith Baca's mural sketch draws a panoramic fuerza.
On the outskirts, police wave their batons—defund them!

All they find is a closet, when lesbians and gays gather
for "The Call" to rebel, organized at the table, arm in arm.

On a transparent plane, gay couples hold each other, when
three identical yet solo men at the bar have faces behind

their heads. "VICE TRAP" on the game by the man who
speaks to the identical face. Lo que fuera afuera es fuerza.

Luto in Protest

*"The 1977 wrongful beating and murder of Vietnam War veteran
Joe Campos Torres by officers from the Houston Police Department
serves as one of the most notorious examples of police misconduct in
the city's history."*

—Jesús Jesse Esparza

Spatial *WE ARE*
THEIR VOICES to show

a hatted hombre in uniform, murió
por ser él mismo. Say his name:

Joe Campos Torres. A veteran
imagen on a poster held

at the 3rd Annual Joe Campos Torres
Solidarity Walk for Past and Future

Generations. Racist police brutality
remembered. Houston Police Department beat

and threw him into Buffalo Bayou with handcuffs.
Remembered. ¡Joe Campos Torres presente!

He died on Cinco de Mayo, cadaver found
on Mother's Day. Since 1977, la familia no puede

festejar. Now in solidarity with Black
Lives Matter. On poster, WHAT

HAPPENS WHEN WE FEAR
FOR OUR LIVES? Parent

and child abrazándose. Monica
Villarreal's printmaking captures

light, shadows, textures, gente
que sólo quiere ser gente.

Los Pueblos Unidos Jamás Serán Vencidos

1

Cardstock, vellum, and tissue paper flutter

                in the shape of moths along the wall edging

hacia las ventanas, a growing migration just

                across the Museum of Contemporary Native Arts.

Latinx artist Paula Castillo's *Yucca Moth*

                Field—Mutualism and Coevolution leads

the hallway in the exhibit *Reconciliation*,

                un espacio donde Latinx and Native artists meet

and decolonize juntes. The yucca moth

                pollinates yucca plants, an interdependence

between fauna and flora, a relationship.

2

Lynette Haozous from Chiricahua Apache,

                    Diné, and Taos Pueblos, connects the ceiling

to the floor *Braiding Reconciliation*: manilla

                    rope, corn stalks, yucca, wool made rope-like,

all braided and twisted with knots similar

                    to those from the Pueblo Revolt in 1680 in an

umbilical cord or a DNA Helix, the height

                    of the room. The gallery became a rebellious womb

against hangings, whippings, dismemberments,

                    and slavery. Stones from various communities in a

wooden basket on the floor, a few rocks

                    netted by the ropes to join forces.

3

Latinx Camilla Trujillo's triptych *Land*
       of Strong Mothers herb wall made of medicinal

herbs and food. "High Healing Desert" has earthy
       tones swirl in a rectangular composition against

 a maroon spiral: juniper (pain), juniper berries
       (prostate), escoba de víbora (pain), horse nettle

(clotting), chamiso (incense), estafiate (tummy ache),
       which are the medicinal. "Night Sky over Espanola"

has muted tones in curved diagonals in a horizontal
       composition: chile (comida), beans (comida), corn

(comida), squash (comida), dandelion greens (diet
       yerba), quelite wild spinach (diet yerba), verdolaga

purslane (diet yerba), rosehips (diet yerba), amole

roots (shampoo), milkweed (treats moles), torito

goathead (tea for pain). "Mountain Healing" is a vertical

composition with an eddy of herbs on top and crisscross

diagonal clusters below: osha (protection from snakes),

yerba manzo (blood tonic), and evergreens (air freshener

and hope giver). Together they heal with movement,

a static capture of harvest in motion.

4

On the wall, painted fresco, powder pigments,

and gum arabic by Deborah A. Jojola from Isleta

and Jemez Pueblos. *Prayer to All My*

Relatives is shaped like an adobe monument,

semi-symmetrical. The image of a centered
                                   pole is almost the height of the fresco

with the top expanding into a globule that curly clouds
                                   cuddled and that an arch crowns

with arrows pointing upward on the ends.
                                   To the left are tall flowers, to the right corn stalks.

Underneath are footprints, paw prints,
                                   and tadpole prints. On the outer sides are decorative

structures with steps, autumn colors
                                   and periwinkle contrast earthy land, building, and sky.

Afar, the figurative forms give a place for
                                   the eye to rest amid the partial symmetry, and up

close the illusional space gives cohesion to
                                   the stucco's physical cracks.

5

Latinx Roger Montoya's *Resolana: The Sun*
Illuminating Our Reflection is a round mirror,

short wooden rays, long yucca-stalk and corn-stalk
rays. The face of the sun is the mirror of your face,

of my face, of our face, de tu cara, de la mía,
de nosotres.

9.

My circle of personal space is smaller than the average U.S. American. I used to get frustrated that people stepped away from me when I approached them. On the other hand, when I worked as a cashier at a restaurant where all the workers hablaban en español, some of the waitresses would stand next to me, touching me. I don't know if it was natural, or if it contributed to the way I was mocked for being queer (one of them put her index finger and middle finger in the shape of a *V* in front of her mouth and then stuck her tongue out at me through the slit of the *V*).

My induction into poetry started at a young age when I listened to lyrics. I loved rock en español as rebellion against my parents' traditions and against mainstream U. S. American music, a borderlands prosody. I think of the senses as a method to communicate in a world of germaphobes who do not like to touch.

Now that there is a pandemic and the norm is to stand six feet away or more, I no longer think that being a germaphobe is exaggerated. Touching air is a risk, a matter of life and death, so contact with another person seems so distant, leaving tactile senses dissatisfied.

I know not to—but some artwork is hermoso, marvelous, mesmerizing; I want to touch it.

Fin

Notes

PAGE 7: *Watcha*'s epigraph is from Pauline Oliveros in her book *Sounding the Margins: Collected Writings 1992-2009*, published by Deep Listening Publications in 2010. I participated in a Deep Listening workshop led by Oliveros toward the end of her life, and it changed my own life.

PAGES 15 & 16: Arlene Dávila's book *Latinx Art: Artists, Markets, and Politics*, published by Duke University in 2020, advocates for Latinx art. By centering what's aural, Oliveros decentered visual communication, but as Dávila has mentioned, Latinx art does not receive the visibility it ought to have. My ideas about Deep Watching and Quantum Watching are derived from a reinterpretation of the book *Sounding the Margins: Collected Writings 1992-2009*, by Oliveros.

PAGE 17: This is a scan of a photograph I took when I was in art school. I developed the film and photograph using a darkroom. When I told my artist friend Lucy Lenoir I was taking a photography course, she gave me a tour of Austin. I believe this is in north Austin.

PAGE 19: The quotations are aphorisms I remember from my professors. I don't recall the sculptor's name, but I remember he disliked my work. The photographer was Lawrence D. McFarland; he encouraged my photography, much of which is in *Watcha*.

PAGE 21: The quotations are from memory, but the ones from the bar must have been all in English, despite the fact that I have memories in Spanish of the xenophobia that occurred the day Whitney Houston passed away.

PAGE 22: This is another photo from when I was in art school. I asked Lucy Lenoir to appear to be crossing the street. I think this is in northeast Austin a couple decades before it became more developed.

PAGE 23: Violette Bule's soap sculpture had the word "HISPANO" branded and was a commentary on the commercialization of the word and its identity markers.

PAGES 24 & 25: Surpik Angelini spoke about Violette Bule at her artist talk for an exhibit I did not see, but I thought that Angelini's words applied to Bule's work in general. The words "in guns we trust" come from Bule's postcard *Slam the Dreamers*.

PAGES 26, 27, 28, & 29: The names of the cities and towns were embroidered in Violette Bule's *Dream la Bestia*. On the fabric, I recognized the image of Eddie Murphy from *Coming to America*.

PAGE 30: The italics are words that immigration officers have asked me when taken to primary, secondary, and tertiary questioning.

PAGE 32: "Don't touch!" are words I heard by a gallery attendant in the Queens Museum. The words "'abduction' by an alien force" were on the didactic placard in the museum, so I figured they were composed by curator Robb Hernández. Arnoldo García and I discussed MacMurtrie via Facebook.

PAGE 34: I had discussions with art historian Ray Hernández-Durán and artist Henry G. Sánchez about Sergio Hernández through Facebook. The word "alien" was the legal term for immigrants in the United States before the it got changed to "noncitizen."

PAGE 35: The quotations come from Laura Drey's produce twist ties.

PAGE 37: "Lourdes Gutiérrez Rosales" was one of the name tags in Nabil Gonzalez's installation. "Ni una más" is a slogan against femicides.

PAGE 38: *Our Lady of the Checkpoint* is the title of a print by Celeste De Luna but is also words embedded into her print, as seen on her website https://www.celestedeluna.com/. The questions in italics are words that immigration officers have asked me when taken to primary, secondary, and tertiary questioning. The "Anzaldúan 'conocimiento'" refers to a consciousness that Gloria Anzaldúa explains in her dissertation *Light in the Dark/Luz en lo oscuro: Rewriting Identity, Spirituality, Reality*, which was published posthumously by Duke University in 2015. I read the Anzaldúan reference in Celeste De Luna's bio at Box 13 during Latino Art Now! 2019, and I immediately recognized the reference.

PAGE 41: I didn't understand "Velouria" by the Pixies from the 1990 album *Bossanova*, so I inadvertently made up my own lyrics, or at least one word. In Houston, Spanish speakers refer to Magnolia Park as "Magnolia."

PAGE 43: This picture was taken in Magnolia Park. The film was developed, and the photo was created at art school. The family whose picture I took was friendly. I was preoccupied thinking about the children. I was considering becoming a bilingual elementary school teacher at the time, and we were next to the elementary school I went to as a child.

PAGES 44, 45, & 46: The first quotation is what Stephanie Saint Sanchez labeled on a television. The rest of the quotations are snippets of recordings from her installation. When I heard the words "I can't breathe," I thought of Eric Garner—it was a year before George Floyd's death. When I asked Sanchez about the words, she said the voice was George Lopez. I found myself searching the Internet looking for the Lopez clip; I recall finding it and not laughing. I closed my eyes when Floyd's murder was televised, and upon hearing the same words, I knew not what to do. A few weeks later, I decided to revise the poem and name both Garner and Floyd.

PAGE 47: The terms *Southern*, *Gulf Coast*, and *Afro-Xicana* were words I read in Leticia Contreras's profile at the Greater Houston Latinx Artist Registry Directory (LARD), better known as MANTECA.

PAGES 50 & 51: The words of the quotations were taken directly from Bianca Mercado's quilt. The slashes indicate line breaks as they were presented on the quilt.

PAGE 53: Judith Baca spoke at an artist talk at the Whitney Museum of American Art via Zoom that took place at dinnertime. I was cooking when Baca spoke, so I was not able to write or quote her, only paraphrase her. My dialog was an exchange I had on a street in Magnolia Park.

PAGE 54: This is the picture I took in Magnolia Park. I developed the film and created the photo in art school. I was still empathizing with the children. In particular, since they were girls and I was once a girl who rode her bike on the Magnolia Park streets, I wondered what would happen to them.

PAGES 55 & 56: The words are fragments of what Laura Aguilar handwrote below her photographs.

PAGES 58 & 59: I used the pachuco dialect I learned from *Zoot Suit* by Luis Valdez, whose play was originally written in 1978, but I read the 1992 version, published by Arte Público Press.

PAGE 61: Gloria Anzaldúa theorizes *nepantla*, a spiritual liminal space, in her dissertation *Light in the Dark/Luz en lo oscuro: Rewriting Identity, Spirituality, Reality*, which was published posthumously by Duke University in 2015.

PAGE 62: This is another photo taken at Magnolia Park but created in art school. I stopped to take a break on my walk home and decided to take a self-portrait.

PAGE 63: The quotation comes from the video Jillian Mayer created.

PAGE 65: The term is theorized by Gloria Anzaldúa in her book *Borderlands/La Frontera*, published by Aunt Lute in 1987.

PAGE 71: The Gloria Anzaldúa quotation comes from her book *Borderlands/La Frontera*, published by Aunt Lute in 1987. *Los caifanes* is a 1967 film written by Carlos Fuentes. Caifanes was a rock band in the 1990s from Mexico. The word *caifanes* originates from 1940s pachuco dialect but found its way to become a transnational word that refers to nonconformists. The Pauline Oliveros quotation comes from her book *Sounding the Margins: Collected Writings 1992-2009*, published by Deep Listening Publications in 2010.

PAGE 73: This is another photo from art school. Lucy Lenoir was going up spiral stairs above me, and I took a picture of her zoomed in.

PAGES 74, 75, & 76: Karen Martínez looped two films (*Nepantla* and *Malinalli*) together. Malinalli is La Malinche's birthname. Nepantla is a concept about a spiritual liminal space that Gloria Anzaldúa theorizes in her dissertation *Light in the Dark/Luz en lo oscuro: Rewriting Identity, Spirituality, Reality*, which was published posthumously by Duke University in 2015. Martínez had the film *Nepantla* in sections: "Intro," "Auto Da Fé," "La Piedad en el Desierto," and "Flor de Jaguar." The film begins with the Elisabet Velasquez quotation. In *Nepantla*, there is a water jug with the words "SIN FRONTERAS."

PAGE 78: Erick Zambrano's sculpture included caution tape, and he told me tagua nuts are called "vegetable ivory."

PAGE 83: The use of quotation marks around "my people" was intended to be scare quotes because I never understood the term. While I was suicidal, I read Electa Arenal and Amanda Powell's translation *The Answer/La Respuesta* by Sor Juana Inés de la Cruz. Their translation was published in 2009 by The Feminist Press. After I came back from the behavioral health hospital, I went to look at my notes to see my thinking, and I saw that my one comment was where Powell and Arenal had translated "dust," which I marked as "pulverized." At the time I wrote it, I thought about being silenced as a form of death.

PAGE 84: This is another art school photo. I was touching my dead chicken I was eating.

PAGE 89: The words in quotation marks were handwritten by Mundo Meza, and I kept the capitalization the way he wrote it.

PAGE 93: The epigraph comes from an interview that Ángel Lartigue posted on Facebook about her artwork.

PAGES 95 & 96: Lartigue's installation entitled *Por los siglos de los siglos* is named after the end of a Catholic prayer, though the exhibit had an image of Coyolxauhqui and had the name "Mictlantecuhtli" in the exhumation maps that Lartigue drew. The words in all caps are quotations that all come from Lartigue's exhumation maps.

PAGE 99: I mention Pauline Oliveros because I describe my process of Deep Listening as praxis.

PAGE 101: This is the only photograph in *Watcha* from when I studied Creative Writing in the Bay Area, where I also took a photography class. The image was taken at the Mission District, a traditionally Latinx neighborhood in San Francisco, but the darkroom was in Oakland. This picture was on the outskirts of the neighborhood, which was starting to become gentrified.

PAGE 102: The quotations come from Judith Baca's drawing.

PAGES 103 & 104: The epigraph comes from Jesús Jesse Esparza's "Kill the Pigs! The Case of Joe Torres and the Fight Against Police Brutality in Houston, 1977-1978," which is a Spring 2023 article in *Southern Studies: An Interdisciplinary Journal of the South*, Special Issue "The Black and Brown Experience in the Bayou City," volume 30, number 1. The epigraph is also a fragment of a sentence in Esparza's "Torres, Joe Campos" in *Handbook of Texas Online*, published by the Texas State Historical Association in April 2022. In my poem, the part about the handcuffs I read in an ABC article by Mayra Moreno entitled "41 Years Later: Remembering Joe Campos Torres' Death by HPD That Sparked Moody Park Riots," published in 2018. When Janie Torres (the sister of Joe Campos Torres) spoke at the Holocaust Museum Houston in 2021 via Zoom, I asked her if the newspaper was correct in reporting the handcuffs. She replied that she had heard both accounts: yes he was in handcuffs as well as no he was not in handcuffs. When the evidence is not conclusive, what is left is belief. What do I believe? I know from Esparza's 2020 presentation for the Oral History Association entitled "Holding Them Accountable: Coalition Building and the Struggle Against Police Misconduct" that Joe Campos Torres was beaten twice, once before he was taken to jail and a second time after the police officers who brought him to jail were ordered to take him to the hospital instead. From Esparza, I also learned that Torres fell seventeen feet into the bayou. I believe the officers intended to kill Torres. Thus, I don't have reason to believe that they ever took the handcuffs off. Monica Villarreal had two posters at Multicultural Education and Counseling through the Arts (MECA) for Latino Art Now! 2019. One entitled *WE ARE THEIR VOICES* was a monochromatic image of Joe Campos Torres with the title of the piece, and the other had a parent and child embracing each other with the words "WHAT HAPPENS WHEN WE FEAR FOR OUR LIVES?" The didactic placard said both were used at the 3rd Annual Joe Campos Torres Solidarity Walk for Past and Future Generations.

PAGES 107 & 108: Camilla Trujillo's *Land of Strong Mothers* was a triptych of "High Healing Desert," "Night Sky over Espanola," and "Mountain Healing." I used the tombstone to name the materials used for the compositions.

PAGE 113: The picture was taken in Houston but processed at art school. It is a picture of my abuelito, whom I'd still like to hug.

Acknowledgments

This poetry would have never been written if it weren't for the many artists whose work inspired me to write *Watcha*. Gracias a elles. In particular, the Houston artists and artists who used to live in Houston all walked me through their artwork, so thank you, Jorge Galván Flores, Stephanie Saint Sanchez, Violette Bule, Ángel Lartigue, Leticia Contreras, Gabriel Martínez, Tina Hernandez, Karen Martínez, Erick Zambrano, Laura Drey, and Monica Villarreal.

My ekphrastic journey began on an art history trip to Mexico with art historian Rex Koontz, and although the poems for that course are not in *Watcha*, I'd like to thank him for encouraging my ekphrasis, for it eventually led me to *Watcha*.

I'd like to thank the eyes that saw earlier iterations of *Watcha*, especially Lorna Dee Cervantes, ire'ne lara silva, Rosebud Ben-Oni, Leslie Contreras Schwartz, Ching-In Chen, Cassie Mira, Aliah Lavonne Tigh, JD Pluecker, Heidi Kasa, and my University of Houston family, including Joshua Gottlieb-Miller, Niki Herd, Roberto Tejada, María C. González, Amanda Ellis, and Cristina Rivera Garza.

I am grateful for my familial support during my artistic development, especially my late mom María Jiménez, my twin brother Carlos Villarreal, and my cousin Luz Rocio Jiménez.

My Nameless Sound family of sonic improvisers helped me develop an ear for the sounds of *Watcha* during readings. Thanks, Ivette Román Roberto, David Dove, Ayanna Jolivet Mccloud, Ryan Edwards, Garbriel

Martínez, Sonia Flores, Anthony Almendárez, Megan Easely, Parham Daghighi, and Justin Jones.

Thanks to giovanni singleton, Samantha Rodriguez, and the late Elliot Harmon for listening to my *Watcha* thought process.

Gracias a Michael Bryan who helped me with the barber lingo in "*Fade Away: Desaparecer*."

Thank you, Jesús Jesse Esparza, for the access to your important work on Joe Campos Torres.

I'd like to thank Ray Hernández-Durán, Henry G. Sánchez, and Arnoldo García for having conversations about Latinx art I examined for *Watcha*.

Thanks to all the people in my photographs: Lucy Lenoir, my abuelito, and kind strangers.

Gracias, Violette Bule, por la author photo.

Thank you to the countless people on social media who helped me with the phrasing of the dedication of this book.

Thanks to Anita Stubenrauch for including the poem "A History Removed" in her podcast *Hyperactive Imagination*.

Thanks to Rodrigo Toscano and Shook for affirming the title *Watcha*.

Thank you to Adrian Matejka for selecting some of the poems in *Watcha* for the Inprint Donald Barthelme Prize in Poetry.

Thanks to Noemi Press for selecting *Watcha* as a finalist for their 2021 Noemi Press Poetry Award.

Thank you to the Deep Vellum team for making this publication possible.

I'd also like to acknowledge the following previous publications of poems in *Watcha*:

Defunkt Magazine: Earlier versions of "Feminicidio fronterizo," "Lo que subsuma Celeste De Luna," and "The Female Gaze Facing the Self: Tina Hernandez Self-Portraiture"

Good Cop/Bad Cop: An Anthology: Earlier version of "Luto in Protest"

The Loop: Earlier versions of "Flooded Memoria" and "Watcha" (originally entitled "Hispano Soap")

Queer Latinx Writers Responding to Here, Ahora: Houston, Latinx, Queer Artists Under 30 at Art League Houston: Earlier version of "Death as a Fashion Statement"

Angel-Lartigue.com: Earlier version of "Death as a Fashion Statement"

The Rupture: "Physical Space of *Bodies of Color Cuerpos de Color*," "Erick Zambrano's Sculptural Composition of Gendered Visceral and Cerebral Abstraction," and "Consciousness y la mestiza"

Superpresent: "Passport Interrogations," "*Invader de Aztlán*," "*Mapping Borders*," and "Chico MacMurtrie and Amorphic Robot Works (ARW)'s Kinetic Tunnel Sculpture"

Biographical Information

Stalina Emmanuelle Villarreal (she/they) sees, hears, feels, and communicates across mediums and cultures. She's a deep-watching ekphrastic poet, a photographic flash essayist, a broad-stroke sketch artist, a sonic improv performer, a sound-sensitive literary translator, and an assistant professor of English. Their bilingualism stems from her 1.5-generation experience being both Mexican and Xicanx. Their poetry can be found in the *Rio Grande Review*, *Texas Review*, the *Acentos Review*, *Defunkt Magazine*, and elsewhere. Their published translations of poetry include *Enigmas* by Sor Juana Inés de la Cruz, *Photograms of My Conceptual Heart Absolutely Blind* by Minerva Reynosa, *Kilimanjaro* by Maricela Guerrero, and *Postcards in Braille* by Sergio Pérez Torres. Stalina is the recipient of the Inprint Donald Barthelme Prize in Poetry. Her visual poetry—spanning queer erotica, interactive digital art, and video installation—was part of the *Antena@Blaffer* exhibit at University of Houston's Blaffer Art Museum. She is currently writing ekphrastic elegies about her interpretative drawings of portraits and a memoir about her photographs of nature—revealing her ability to look backward and within, to write new ways forward.